Telling Tales

D1147305

TELLING
TALES

A collection of short stories, poetry
and drama, by writers from adult
basic education.

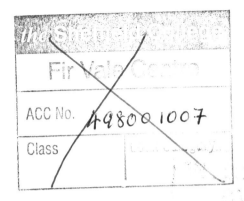
First published in 1992 by Gatehouse Books.

The Gatehouse Publishing Charity Ltd
Birley Centre, Chichester Road,
Manchester M15 5FU

Gatehouse is grateful for continued financial support from Manchester City Council, Manchester Adult Education Service, and North West Arts Board, and for financial assistance towards the production of this book from The Reader's Digest Trust.

Typeset in avant garde by Arena Design, Ferguson House,
11 Blackfriars Road, Manchester M3 7DN.
Printed by The Manchester Free Press, M4 6FP
Photographs: Marian Keen

British Library Cataloguing In Publication Data:
Telling Tales: Collection of Short Stories, Poetry and Drama from Writers in Adult Basic Education 820.914008

ISBN 0 906253 34 9

Gatehouse is a member group of the Federation of Worker Writers & Community Publishers.

CONTENTS

Contents contd.

LINE BREAKING

We have designed the book
to make it useful
to people who don't find reading easy.
Some stories
are broken into short lines like this,
so you can take a break
at a point that makes sense.

A TALE

Telling Tales is a special book.

Its tales are written by people in adult basic education. They tell their stories with skill, imagination and feeling, to make you smile or maybe a little sad. *Telling Tales* aims to reach other people who are interested in writing: as individuals, as students and tutors in adult basic education, as people in writing groups and as students and teachers in schools. As well as giving you a good read, it aims to encourage you and get you started on a piece of writing. Many of the writers tell us what writing is like for them, or how they came to write their story, poem or play. You'll also find other sections written especially to writers. Look out for this sign ‡.

Stories are going on inside us and around us all the time. We make them up about people we hardly know, gathering hints from their clothes, behaviour, conversations, to add to our knowledge. People we meet on the bus, at college, in the pub. We are surprised sometimes when we find out something that doesn't fit in with the story we make up about them, for ourselves. We watch and listen to stories on television and radio through plays, films, soap operas. It's how we make sense of our lives and what goes on around us. It's one way we can share feelings, pleasures, truths with other people. But when we write stories down, we share them with many more people.

1

In *Telling Tales* some writers have used their memories, trying to get some distance on what happened in order to shape it for us, the readers (especially Anne Comrie, Mary Corr, Marie Duffy, Doreen Kirven, Tommy McKee, Sheilagh Tynan). Other writers have taken a piece of experience and have found ways to open it out so that we can find something of ourselves there (especially Carole Chandlett, Peter Goode, Victor Grenko, Vivienne Sparkes). Other writers have begun from what they know, but have used other influences, other models, to shape a tale for us (especially Mary Buckley, Kathleen Byrne, Bill Lunn, Carol Millbanks, Laurence Roper, The 21 Hour Group).

Do you have to always tell the truth when you write? Isn't truth very difficult to pin down anyway? An accurate account of what happened in our lives is important for a life-experience story or autobiography, but how accurate can we ever be? One person's version of what happened may vary from another person's, yet both of them feel they are being truthful. Is it okay to 'launch off' from and add to what actually happened to make the story interesting for readers? Isn't every story we tell a useful insight into how we all live our lives?

Telling Tales isn't a collection of life-stories, but it is a collection of poems-plays-stories-from-life. They are all 'tales'. A tale can be a 'true' story or completely made up.

Tales like Tommy McKee's *Rat In A Trap* and *A Drop Of The Hard Stuff* come from a spoken tradition which is part of Tommy's Celtic heritage. His Irishness shows through the way he uses language. It helps some people to imagine an Irish accent when they read the story.

Victor Grenko's *The Snow Queen* reverses the convention of spring being wonderful and winter merely cold, useless water. In this tale spring comes because it follows winter.

Mary Buckley's *Double Life* shows us that creative writing can be a successful part of exam preparation. See Mary's 'afterword' on page (39).

All these tales have been very carefully worked and re-worked by the writers, with Gatehouse giving support. Writing takes a lot of thought and effort. Most of us need to try two, or three, or more times before the words seem right. Inside on pages (29) and (87) you'll see two of these early struggles to make the words say what the writer wants them to say. Thanks to Kathleen Byrne and Peter Goode for letting us show *how the writing looked at first*. Once writing is printed, it looks so organised and professional. All signs of the early struggle disappear. It's good to remind ourselves that this is what it's like at first for all of us. For example here's what my early struggle to write this bit looked like:

Talking is an important part of writing. It's the part that goes on before the writing, that helps to get it out of our head and down on paper. A lot of discussion has gone on around this writing. A group of people met fortnightly over the course of a year at Gatehouse, for a process of reading, talking and selecting from the writing sent in for *Telling Tales*. They are writers and tutors themselves, so they know of the effort and thought that went into every piece of writing they considered. They made careful choices for the book over a period of time. Gatehouse is grateful to them. Editorial work is a two-way process, because as well as using skills, you learn new ones and often grow as a writer yourself.

As Kathleen Byrne writes on page (91) everyone can write. You don't have to be able to spell, or to hold a pen in order to get ideas down on paper. Ask another person to be a 'right hand' for you, or maybe use a tape recorder while you're finding the words, then take your time and write them down yourself. If you have ideas you want to get to other people, put them on paper and when you're ready, give them to others to read.

Enjoy Telling Tales!

Stella Fitzpatrick
March, 1992

The Editorial Group:
Clockwise from left: Eddie Quayle, Chris Barrett, Vivienne Sparkes, Thelma Banks, Stella Fitzpatrick, Doris Thelfall, Tommy McKee, Sue Batt. Bill Lunn (not in photo).

YOU NEVER KNOW THE VALUE TILL YOU SEE THE VACANT CHAIR

Sheilagh Tynan

Life was very hard for Winnie.
Her mother was an alcoholic.
Many times the children were cold and hungry,
And pawnshops were the order of the day.
Winnie missed a lot of schooling
With seven brothers and sisters to look after
When Mother was 'ill'.
When things were bad, she would curl up in her chair
And 'think'.
Winnie learned at an early age to be a survivor.

As a young woman
Winnie worked in the grocery trade.
She went for her first job interview.
To get the job,
She said she had worked in a shop before.
She was asked to cut and weigh a piece of cheese.
She cut it with wires,
Dropped it on the scales
And it was exactly right!
She got the job.
In later years, she managed several shops.
She loved the work,
Because through it, she met people.

But the war was on,
There was very little time to sit in her chair.

When she married, in her mid-twenties,
Winnie made her home a safe place;
She was there.
It was full of activity, chatter,
Humour and laughter,
Sometimes tears.
The smells of cooking and polish ...
Washing neatly ironed ...
Lost items found, on her chair,
Where she solved problems with wisdom
And gave caution with gentle listening
And warm embracing,
Often spilling beyond the bounds of family
Into the local community,
And never a confidence broken.

In her old age, after much suffering,
Which again she survived,
Winnie's chair became a wheelchair.
Her grandchildren bought her cushions for it,
A nice rug.
She was still her own person,
And a force to be reckoned with.
Winnie could still love and share a laugh
And talk to everybody.

She never lost her sense of humour
Or her dignity.
The richness of her character
Influenced so many people.
But the greatest strength she had
Was her faith. That, and her family
Kept her going.
But now, she was very tired ...

You never know the value till you see the vacant chair.

Sheilagh Tynan

Photo: Marian Keen

I am an auxiliary nurse and am married to James who is also a nurse. We have three grown up children.

I am involved with my local church and enjoy going to the ladies group and the amateur dramatic society. I decided to enrol at the nearby adult education centre and take a course in English. I like writing when I have time. I wrote a short piece of work about my mother which Gatehouse came across. This opportunity has given me great encouragement.

‡ *How important is 'the chair' to the way Sheilagh has constructed this story?*
Is this a real life story? How does Sheilagh make her mother's life into a tale? How does she get some distance on it and shape it, so as to tell a whole life in a page and a half?
Does Sheilagh's selection from her memories work to build a word-picture for you?

10

ROYAL SAGA

Carole Chandlett

A beautiful princess
was locked away in a castle
by her wicked step-father.
She could only look out of the window
and wait for help to come.

Twenty years later,
a charming prince came riding by
and broke down the door.
Inside the room he found
a most beautiful skeleton.

Anthea Helliwell

11

LLAN DYFED LIGHTHOUSE

Vivienne Sparkes

The sea was calm. The billowing rhythm of the waves slopped the craggy cliffs below and seagulls screamed and dived. The lighthouse stood on a remote island three kilometres off the west coast of Wales. Through its windows I could see with my binoculars, the fishing village and a tangle of masts and rigging from the boats and trawlers which were docked along the bulwarks that extended out into the sea like long, black fingers. I returned the binoculars to the leather case and placed them on the oak dressing table. Silently and carefully I descended the narrow stone spiral staircase and walked across the lounge and into the kitchen, which would have been claustrophobic if the walls had been painted in any colour except white. Meredith my sister, who was a year younger than myself, was making a cup of coffee.

"I'm going over to the village to have a look round. Do you want to come?"

"No, I had a look yesterday when we arrived."

Meredith followed me to the front door.

"What time will you be back because I'll cook tea tonight."

"I'll be back around five o'clock."

I negotiated the step into the boat, untied her and started the outboard motor. Meredith waved goodbye.

I arrived half an hour later. The village seemed deserted. I had expected to find it as it was when we arrived yesterday from Bristol. Walking slowly, I noticed that all the shops I had passed were closed. I suspected that it was some sort of holiday that we had not been informed of. I carried on past the Seaman's Mission where I turned off and up a steep, narrow street. Halfway up and across the street I noticed a tea shop with its door open. I decided to go in. At a table in the corner a man dressed in a navy blue coat, creamy white polo neck jumper and black trousers which were tucked down his wellington boots, was rummaging through a drawstring bag.

I walked over and sat adjacent to him. His grey, thinning hair was neatly cut and brushed regimentally off his chalky white round face. The waitress arrived with her pad and pencil. I watched the middle-aged man pull out a long hardback brown book from another bag and place it gently on the table as I waited for my cup of tea. I craned my neck and leaned over slightly to see the cover, which had an anchor and lighthouse embossed upon it. Underneath this there was a name, Mr Rowe, Lighthouse Keeper. Before I could read more he picked the book up and placed it back into his bag. He looked at me with his small, brown eyes and faintly smiled.

"I haven't seen you in the village before?" he enquired.

"No, my sister and I are taking a weekend break from the city."

"Where are you from?" he asked inquisitively.

"Bristol."

I took a sip of my tea and hesitantly said, "There's a terrible musty smell in here!"

I turned round to signal to the waitress and when I turned back he had gone. I paid my bill and headed back to the lighthouse. The boat buffeted on the waves and my cheeks were numb with the cold. I carefully approached the mooring and tied the boat to a thick wooden stump. I ran up the steps and down the path and opened the front door to a strong smell of bolognaise. I slipped my coat off and went into the kitchen where Meredith was busily cooking our tea. The warmth made my cheeks tingle back to life.

"It's a good thing you're late, I was busy reading and I forgot the time, so tea will be a few more minutes."

By the time I had laid the table and brushed my hair and told Meredith about the middle-aged man, tea was ready. After tea we settled in for the evening. Meredith sat on the settee. Her long legs were placed upon the coffee table and her chestnut hair dangled over her bright green jumper. She began to read. I went over to the bookcase which stood by the side of an old radio and hand set. I picked up a book and flicked through its pages. Tired and uninterested, I decided to go to bed.

The moon was directly outside my window, its light flooding my bedroom and the stars winked and stared against a cloudless black, velvet sky.

Later that evening the tranquility that I had known was suddenly broken by a violent storm. Rain spat harshly against the window, the wind rushed around and over the lighthouse and the waves crashed fiercely against the cliffs. Meredith burst into the bedroom.

"Judith! Judith!" She was shaking violently.

"Can you hear them?" she nervously said.

"Hear what?"

"Sh ..... that. The voices," she whispered.

Meredith sat close to me clasping my arm with her long, bony fingers. The icy cold air made me shiver and I felt a deep uneasiness. Suddenly there was a loud, repetitive pounding on the front door. We stayed huddled together until it stopped and we could only hear the waves booming on the cliffs and the rain pattering on the window. I moved cautiously towards the light switch and turned the light on which started to flicker intermitently. We sat there until day-break.

When we reached the bottom of the stairs the stone floor in the lounge was wet and there was a strong,

musty odour mingled with the smell of salt. It was the smell which I had noticed in the tea shop. It had vanished when the middle aged man had. The books in the lounge were scattered everywhere. I picked my way across to the kitchen and on the table lay the book I had seen at the tea shop. I opened it and thumbed the pages. It was an old log book. I shouted to Meredith and I read the last entry to her. *September 29th, 1938. Three o'clock. A trawler has struck the cliffs. Mr Rowe from Llan Dyfed Lighthouse and all hands on board the trawler, Fisherman's Wake, have been lost. Signed, Samuel Jones.*

Meredith and I stood silently together, our eyes questioningly looking at the book and then at each other. Meredith broke the silence.

"Was this the book you saw yesterday at the tea shop? Did I hear voices, or was it the sea ....?"

Vivienne Sparkes

Photo: Marian Keen

WHAT WRITING IS LIKE FOR ME

Vivienne Sparkes

A few words that create an image or an atmosphere will start me off writing, if it's something that I really feel strongly about. I walk up and down, drink coffee, smoke a lot, thinking of what to write, that perfect phrase.

Llan Dyfed Lighthouse came about after reading a few dismembered lines, an extract in a book. In the story I'm drawing on the traditional ghost story but saying something else as well. I wanted to draw women going out, being independent, having experience and adventure. My story is not about looking at a woman and seeing only one facet of her. The women in this story can be separate women, they can be both sides of one woman. Women are usually excluded from places like lighthouses, so I put us there, doing and being what we want. The combination of women's names, Judith and Meredith, gives the story a period feel, saying hopefully that women have always gone out into the world, having a great many positive and negative experiences.

I did about three drafts of *Llan Dyfed Lighthouse*, and came down to a final fourth one. I had so many different ideas that once I started writing, I kept having to go back and put something in the margin or scribble out a line and put another line on top. I have an ongoing process of writing the basic story, but keep getting lots and lots of ideas. Finally I try to stop having the ideas and sort out to have one decent story that won't fall flat in the middle. Keeping it moving is important. When I've sorted out the one good idea and the action, I go back and read very slowly and start changing – making a description better, a character more vivid.

It took about a month from the first idea to the final draft. I wanted to perfect it. Even now, I'm not satisfied with it. There comes a point when you've got to say, "I'm never going to be totally satisfied". Off and on I worked on it, intensively at first, then in spurts and spasms. When I get to a certain stage, I won't work as hard. I'll let it simmer in my own mind. Some ideas you get won't work out. They're too complicated and you have to simplify them.

‡*Viv returned to study in 1986. She was on the fringes of the group that year, shy and unconfident. She has tons of talent, but she is the last person to be aware of this. Always good at giving support to other people, she did a lot of word processing work towards a book that her group was producing. Slowly, she began to gain in confidence and her own writing began to blossom. She gained a lot from a writing weekend with Gatehouse. Currently, with GCSE's and A levels behind her, Viv is hoping to begin a degree course.*

RAT IN A TRAP

Tommy McKee

One Sunday when I was twelve years old, I went to see an aunt and uncle. I did some work in the garden for them and they told me that they had a rat in a trap. Would I carry the trap into the field for them and their wee terrier dog would finish the rat off? They said that they had to go into town to do some shopping. Would I stop and look after the house until they got back?

When my aunt and uncle had gone, I finished the garden job first and then I went over to the rat trap. There was a big rat in it. I lifted the trap and it was too heavy for me. I thought, I am not carrying that trap away out into the field where the dog would catch it easy. I will just let the rat out here in the garden. I knew the dog had not got a good chance of catching the rat, as the hedges were just a few yards away. So, I decided to get a big stick, thinking maybe I could open the trap door with one hand, and have the other hand with the stick ready to come down on the rat as it was coming out of the trap. The dog was ready too. I opened the trap door and the rat came out. I came down hard with the stick, the dog sprang in at the same time, and I hit the dog and the rat got away! The dog let an awful yap out of him and I thanked God I had not killed him. The dog was friendly with me after, so he must have thought it was the rat that got him. Then my aunt and uncle came home and they could see a big black mark on the dog. They asked me what had happened. I told them that the rat bit the dog, and got away. My aunt just said, "I believe you, but there are thousands that would not. You see Tommy, all the neighbours round here come for our dog when they have a rat in their trap, and there is not one rat that got away yet!"

I stopped another hour or two with them and I had a very nice tea, and ice cream after. Just as we had finished our tea, there was a knock on the door and it was a young girl from next door. She wanted the dog as there was a rat in their trap. My aunty said to me, "Here is a chance for you to see just how good the dog is."

I walked out into the field with the girl and the dog. She let the rat out of the trap and the dog just walked away. I ran after the rat and killed it. My aunty gave me two shillings and the man next door gave me six pennies for killing the rat. I said, "I am going home now and I think you need a new dog." Sometimes a dog decides he has had enough and he won't catch any more. I thanked them very much and I bid them goodbye.

Tommy McKee

Photo: Marian Keen

A wee bit about myself.

Born in Glasgow. Went to Ireland at a very young age.
I was in Ireland about twenty five years. Then I went to
Rochdale. I was over seventy years when I went to the
Rochdale College. As well as *Rat In A Trap* and *A Drop
Of The Hard Stuff,* I have written two bigger stories. I am
hoping to have some luck with them.

‡*Tommy's way of telling stories comes from a 'spoken tradition'. You
imagine you could as easily hear the story, as read it. Is the writing
really like speech? How carefully do you think Tommy has worked
on the language of his story since he first 'spoke' it?*

*Do you think this story shows how we can turn what really happens
to us into fiction? Is there such a thing as 'a born story teller' or are
there hidden 'rules' that some people operate when they tell a
story? Can you find any 'rules for storytelling' operating in this story,
or in Tommy's other story, **A Drop Of The Hard Stuff**?*

23

A DROP OF THE HARD STUFF

Tommy McKee

When I was twelve years old, which was about sixty years ago, I was living in a little village in Northern Ireland. One day I was going into town on my bike. An old lady asked me if I would take a bottle into the doctor's for her. The bottle was full, with a whiskey label on it. I told her I would take it in for her. She put the bottle in an old shopping bag. I thought she must be keeping in with* the doctor and he will be looking after her with bottles of medicine and tablets and so on.

In the old days, people going into town went into the cathedral to say a few prayers, and that is what I did. I left the bag on the back seat and I walked up to the front and I said a few prayers that I might get to heaven one day. On my way out I lifted the bag and I was horrified. Someone had stolen the bottle! I ran out and there was a policeman coming on his bike. I shouted at him to stop and I told him what had happened. He said, "I will have a look around a few streets and I might find someone drunk. That whiskey is very strong stuff and very expensive. It's about twelve shillings and six pence a bottle." The policeman came back about five minutes later and I could see by the look on his face, he must have caught someone. He told me it was not whiskey that was in the bottle and

*Keeping in with: showing favour to someone so they will show favour to you.

24

Ian Hering

that there was a very sick man just around the corner
with the bottle broken. He was afraid to move. It was
a bottle of urine, a sample for the doctor. You see in
the old days there was no national health service so

people just put samples in any old bottle they could find. The policeman said, "There might be some good come out of this case, because that man would fight with his own grandmother when he has drink inside him. He is the type that goes home and is nasty with his wife and children. Maybe this will cure him."

The policeman took my name because he said one never knows what effect this might have on the man. He said, "You have had enough for one day. Just go home and tell the old lady the doctor wants another sample which you could bring in tomorrow, and say nothing to anyone about what happened."

Next day the old lady was pleased that the doctor wanted another sample for she could see the doctor taking interest in her case. She gave me two shillings, which was a lot of money sixty years ago. I started off to town feeling happy with myself, but the happiness did not last long. I fell off the bike and the bottle was broken. I carried on into town and I bought a bottle at a pub for a penny. I filled the bottle myself and I thought, the doctor won't know who filled it. A nice girl took the bottle off me at the doctor's, and I told her it was a sample from the old lady, giving her name. The girl said, "Not her again! You see she's always sending samples in and there is nothing wrong with her. We just empty her sample down the toilet." Then her face changed. "This bottle is still warm. You must have filled it yourself!" She said, "Get on your bike and clear off before I tell the doctor!" When I got home, I told the old lady her sample was alright, that the doctor was pleased with it. She said, "Good. I will have another one ready for you next week."

‡Being Irish, Tommy talks and tells stories differently from an English person. His way of telling tales comes from a 'spoken tradition'. It's almost as if you're hearing the story instead of reading it. As if Tommy expects you to respond as you go through it.

If you are from a culture with a strong spoken tradition, how much will you need to change the language when it comes to putting your story on the page? Speaking a story is a different kind of storytelling. Once the story is written, you don't need all the repetitions that we often use in speech. However, you might want to add more background information since we don't have the nods, signs and facial expressions that stand in place of words when the story is spoken. Thinking about these changes isn't about making your story better, it's about making it work better on the page.

In your opinion, what is the important discovery in the second paragraph of Tommy's story? Would you agree that the order in which things happen is vital to good story-plotting? What are the other surprises in store as the story proceeds? Are these 'shifts' important to our sense of satisfaction at the end of the story?

Do you have 'a good yarn' you could develop into a story?

THE CAVE DWELLERS

Peter Goode

After the feasting
and the fullness of spirit,
we passed stories round the circle,
picking each moment
like a piece of tender meat
and wanting to share it
with someone special.

Around the circle
the word goes,
where it stops
nobody knows.
Around the circle the word goes,
where it stops
nobody knows,
for the poem
has yet
not been conceived.

I pick the bone from the ribs
to score on the cave
the meaning of words.
You can trace your eyes
across the cave drawing
to see the colour,

to trace the depth of shape
and its fuller shape.

Even then the sight is impaired.

I learn with each
a new colour and depth
I find I can add
to my own ....

I have got all the words out of the way
like wrapping paper
to see the gift of freedom
to find my own colour.

aftar The fiestng
and The fonas ov
Speret we Past Stores
Ran The Secl Picing
ehc momat Lac a Pes
ov Tetlr wet and woteing
To Ser-it wihc sow win
Rad The Secl The wad
Gos wer it Stops no Batle
nou aRad The Secl The

How the writing looked at first. As you read the printed word, you might
forget about the first struggle to put the ideas in our heads down on paper.

Peter Goode

Photo: Marian Keen

I came to basic education late in life without any skills of reading or writing. I could write my name and that was all. Now I can't imagine the world without writing, it's changed my life so much.

WHAT WRITING IS LIKE FOR ME
Peter Goode

I've always considered myself a story teller. You store the knowledge of past history. You absorb an image within the mind and then it's as free as you want to make it. I describe what I see and I don't question the image. Although I work with a 'right hand' the interpretation is always through my own pair of eyes. In my early writing I would give the world twenty images to say "This is Peter". Now I'm giving one image and somehow it's fuller, it has a beginning, a middle and an end.

I see the actual physical pattern a piece of writing draws. It is a drawing to me. I believe the spirit lives within that shape and I set it free and then you see it. And I'll try this or that rhythm beat. You put two words, three words together and they make music. I will actually abandon words because they don't fit, the song inside me is so important. It might take me two or three days to read my poem as you do, but I know the shape and rhythm, and where the pauses are.

It's like a miracle happens every time someone reads something that I write. I have information, I get a piece of paper and we pass it round. I haven't said a word

31

and yet everybody knows my message as though I've said it in a big loud voice.

‡*Peter Goode's creative inner world gets onto the page in 'Gobbledegook' – his tries at translating the language in his head into written words. He prefers to work with a 'right hand', a person who can scribe, or read with him what he has written and together claim it back for him off the page.* **The Moon On The Window**, *his book of poems, was published in 1989. Peter has contributed writing to two other Gatehouse publications,* **Opening Time**, *a resource pack about writing, and* **Yes, I Like It**, *a poetry book. Peter Goode has received a writer's award from Yorkshire Arts Association.*

What is your interpretation of **Cave Dwellers**?
Are different interpretations possible?

Peter's work shows that you don't have to be able to write and spell to work with the world of imagination, experience and emotion. However, you might want to have a right hand or maybe a tape recorder to help get your words down on paper.

"The right hand is the first step to freedom. You can use stepping stones to climb to your own freedom. It's more fruitful in this way. I've had a taste of the other way, the 'cat sat on the mat' attitude" *(Peter).*

Peter co-led a writing workshop for Gatehouse, with Gillian Frost. **Cave Dwellers** *is linked to Doreen Kirven's* **My Mother** *because both pieces of writing were begun during this workshop.*

MY MOTHER

Doreen Kirven

He (their father) was strict, drank
And frightened us.
Up at six – started work at 6.30.
She lost a boyfriend in the war.
The flu' epidemic was wiping out
Whole families – a sister died,
She was only twenty one.
He (her husband) wiped off her lipstick,
She said –
I'm a scivvy for you all,
Why should I get dressed up?
I wish I was dead.

One day she put ribbons in her hair,
It was too late
She was dying.

Doreen Kirven

Photo: Marian Keen

I became closer to my mother as I got older, especially when I became a mum. I began to see her for herself. I made an effort to develop our relationship. I felt that as a grandparent, she relaxed and allowed herself to enjoy life in a way she had not allowed herself before.

A few months before she died of cancer, she found some ribbons whilst in the hospital and when we arrived for visiting, she had them in her hair. The effect was very startling. It frightened my sister and she made her take them out. To me it was her last gesture of defiance.

Like many people, I carry inside me ideas and memories which are important to me, things I tell myself I'll set down some day, when work and family allow. Since the women's writing group I was in stopped meeting, I haven't written much. We should allow ourselves the time and space to set things down, but there's never an opportunity. A writing workshop organised by Gatehouse, gave me my opportunity. That's when I wrote *My Mother*. I was able to put into the poem some of the powerful and symbolic memories I have of my mother, especially during her last illness.

‡Doreen's poem shows how our real lives inform the stories, plays and poems we write. Do you find it moving? Sad? She gives us certain short bits of information, from the memories she carries. From these we build a picture. Selecting which ideas to use and which to leave out is an important part of the process of writing. Too little information is frustrating and not helpful. Too much makes the writing less interesting, because there's not enough space for the reader to use their imagination and experience. How do you decide?

*Doreen's role within basic education is as a tutor. She wrote **My Mother** during Peter Goode's co-run writing workshop. Who is the tutor and who the student when adults with experience are working together?*

DOUBLE LIFE

Mary Buckley

Mr Edward Cecil Bradshaw lived alone in a tiny bedsit just off Peckham Road. He was quite an ordinary person, or was he? The people who worked with him at Jowett, Jowett and Higgins, thought so. To them he was a nice enough chap, a bit on the fussy side, but solid. After the incident, Mr Vickers his boss, had this to say about him:

"He arrived for work at 8.45am. precisely every morning. He was always meticulously dressed, pin stripe suit, white shirt, black bowler hat, etc. and his work was always done correctly and neatly."

His landlady Mrs Jenkins said, "He was the perfect tenant. Never any trouble or complaints and he always paid his rent on time".

None of them ever suspected that Edward Cecil Bradshaw led another life. None of them knew that from Saturday evening to Sunday evening he became 'Eddy the raver', the rock-n-roll idol. Every Saturday morning Edward would take his case from on top of the wardrobe, pack his things and tell Mrs Jenkins that he was off to see his mother.

He would then go to Peckham Rye Station and catch

a train to wherever there was a rock-n-roll festival. Once there, Eddy would come to life. Blue drainpipe trousers, green jacket with black velvet trims and of course, his blue suede shoes. The girls would scream, shout and swoon when he arrived on stage. He could take them into dreamland with his voice and send shivers down their spine, when he swung his hips. He was the best there was on the rock-n-roll scene since "The King".

Then, come Sunday morning, he would make his way back to Peckham Road. He was really enjoying his double life. He felt he had the best of both worlds, his real world and his dream world.

Everything was fine until that fatal Saturday night. All had gone well. He was a hit again. The newspapers and TV were there. He had performed brilliantly. Then, just as he was leaving the stage, a crowd of girls broke through the barrier and grabbed him. They pulled at his hair and tore at his clothes. They were like animals. Before long, the police were there trying to pull them off, without much success.

All of a sudden, the crowd parted. At first all was quiet and then there was a titter, then another. Before long, the whole hall was ringing with laughter because there he stood, their pop idol. A slightly plump little man with just a wisp of hair on his head, in his Y-fronts, his corset bursting at the seams.

Mary Buckley

Photo: Marian Keen

When I went to college, I was surprised at the different people there. I found that like me, they had it all up top and knew what they wanted to say, but couldn't put it down on paper.

Double Life started off as 'a description of a man' for a piece of work at college. I tried really hard to do the description, but I just couldn't get it. I wanted to do R.S.A. English and this was part of my training for the exam. I found that trying to write a story was the only way to do the description. And so I wrote *Double Life*.

‡*Did* **Double Life** *make you smile? Did it make you wince? Why? Mary uses the fantasy lots of us share, about another exciting life for ourselves, for her character, Edward Cecil Bradshaw. Is she gently poking fun at rock stars? Is the contrast between the lifestyles of Edward Cecil Bradshaw and Eddy the Raver important to the success of the story?*

SAM'S CAP
Marie Duffy

Sam's cap was his yardstick, his barometer and his constant companion. Not so much that it told of the weather or signalled warmth or cold, nor even the temperature of Sam ... No! It was there, sitting firmly on his head for a purpose. It registered Sam's independence, his determination, his awareness and most of all, his aliveness.

When I tell you that Sam's hat sat on his head whilst the rest of him was clad in pyjamas covering his well-scrubbed, but fatally sick body lying under the sheets of the first bed in the men's surgical ward, you may have some idea of its importance to Sam.

He had been delivered to us by ambulance that morning, accompanied by a note from his doctor explaining that Sam was in pain and showing symptoms of a grave internal disorder.

When I first saw him, Sam had been diagnosed, bathed and prepared, and was ready to be wheeled to the theatre. Sister was at the bedside wringing her hands, two young nurses were trying to hide and two male orderlies were pleading with Sam. A very important doctor was waiting, a specially brought-in anaesthetist was said to be getting impatient and a full theatre staff were on hand and being held up. No matter. Sam's mind was firmly made up. He would not budge. He had given up his letter, his pension book, his dirt, modesty and pride but, come hell or high water, he'd be damned if he would give up his cap.

He was going nowhere without it. He never had and he wasn't going to start now. He'd been admitted wearing it, been bathed, put to bed and interviewed by the doctor wearing it, and if the job had to be done, they could either wheel him to theatre with his cap, or get the rest of his clothes and let him out of there.

In Sam's words, unless they wanted his guts to burst all over the bed, they had better get a move on. He couldn't see what all the fuss was about. The parts that needed sorting out were at the other end. His cap should make no difference.

Washing her hands of the whole affair, Sister gave in. I never did get to know how the theatre staff received Sam. I only know that the surgeon never batted an eyelid when he met Sam's look of challenge, but got on with the job of reversing Sam's colon to the outside from its intended place inside ...... the better to watch it and heal it. Whether Sam's well-oiled, battered old cap was removed or covered in the cause of hygiene when the merciful anaesthetic took hold, I do not know, but neither would Sam.

He was received back into the ward with exposed colon, toothless but gowned .... and hatted. He was fast asleep, but with a hint of satisfaction in the jaunt of his cap.

Each day Sam seemed to be a little better and each day the cap sat at a slightly more jaunty angle. When he awoke in the morning it was pulled right over his eyes. It was pushed a bit further up with each passing hour. The degree of tilt showed how Sam was progressing. It showed his desire to sleep when he tired, by slipping down his forehead until it reached just past his eyebrows, where it started off a gentle snore.

We grew to love Sam. He rarely spoke to any of us, but his eyes and his cap showed his gratitude for every little thing that was done for him.

One day, after reporting for duty, a new sister issued my orders. "Help Nurse Jones to lay out Mr Tongue". I had to ask where Mr Tongue was, as I had not met that particular patient. I went to the third bed on the right, as directed ... and stopped dead in my tracks. Sam's bed. They must have moved him to make way for Mr Tongue. I went to the curtained bed and there, hanging on the corner of the floral screen was an oily, scruffy, deserted cap.

With tears in my eyes and an ache in my heart, I helped to prepare Sam for his last journey. I prayed for his soul and remembered that to be at peace, Sam would need his cap.

I took it from the screen and put it near Sam's hand. I swear it had recovered some of its jaunt, it didn't look quite so scruffy, looked a bit more perky, not dejected any more. As though it belonged.

Marie Duffy

Photo: Marian Keen

I am a conventional type, happily married with a family of five children, all grown. Rearing them kept me too busy to commit anything to paper except birthday cards, letters to teachers, and so on.

Sam's Cap comes from a true experience during my stint as an auxiliary nurse. It was one of the many extra duties taken on to provide cash in the lean years of the growing family.

I retired from work seven years ago and joined a writers' workshop and an English "O" level class, and started to write a book of my childhood memories, which I will one day finish. All the story is there, complete in my head. Seven paragraphs are on paper and my new year resolution is to sit down and complete it.

Meanwhile, I write short stories, some poetry. I also co-ordinate a group of writers known as the Eccles Library Writers' Group, who meet in Eccles, near Manchester. We have just produced a book of Tales and Reminiscences of Eccles which we are planning to launch for the occasion of the Eccles Centenary.

‡*Marie concentrates on one character only. She mixes humour and sadness in order to get our interest and sympathy for Sam. She raises our hopes for his health, before lowering them again. She uses Sam's cap cleverly, as a symbol which links each part of her story. She tells us the story as though we, her readers, are a close friend she is confiding in. Do you agree?*

You'll notice how our jobs and experiences, become a part of what we write about.

THOUGHTS IN A DREAM
Bill Lunn

As he came to the bottom of the stairway into the hall, a large, brown envelope with the local General Hospital's stamp on it came through the letterbox and landed on the hall mat by his feet. Must be the results of my test mused Tony to himself. He had been having chest pains for some time now and had managed to take some time off from work where he was a manager at the local bank, to have some tests done at the hospital. As he was so busy at the bank he had asked the doctor if it would be possible to send the results of the tests directly to him. The doctor had not been very happy about this but nevertheless complied with Tony's wishes.

"It's probably only muscular pain anyway," Tony remembered himself saying to the doctor.

He sat down at the kitchen table and read the letter. When he'd finished, he let the letter drop slowly to the table.

"Cancer," he said to himself in a whisper. He felt a shudder run through his body. Even saying the word frightened him.

How can it be cancer for God's sake, I'm only thirty five. It's probably a mistake, they make them all the time. I read a case only recently in the newspaper about this bloke who had been told he had cancer only to be told a month later that the doctor had made a mistake. I'll get onto the hospital, that's what I'll do, get it all sorted out, nothing to panic about, it's just a mistake that's all.

Tony phoned the hospital and, after quite a while hanging on, was asked if he could come into the hospital and see Doctor Dawson as they didn't discuss cases over the phone. He agreed to see the Doctor later that morning.

It wasn't a mistake, he did have cancer. What was he going to do? Six months at the most to live, the doctor had told him. He also told him that when Tony had become aware of the pains in his chest a long time ago, he should have got medical advice at once. If he had done this he just might have been curable. But it was too late now, nothing could be done now.

"Why me?" asked Tony out loud. He laughed to himself bitterly. Isn't that what everyone asks when something like this happens? A lot of people also just lay down on a hospital bed and stayed there until they died, taking bottles of pills everyday to stop the pain; nothing else to do but think about when they were going to die. Well he wasn't going to do any of that. The doctor had suggested that he should come into the hospital whenever the pain had become too unbearable, but he was having none of that. If he was going to die in six months he wanted to enjoy what life he had left. Thank God I don't have a wife and kids to break the news to, he thought. I don't think I could have handled that. I mean what do you say to your wife? "Sorry, love, I've only got six months to live. Better make sure the insurance is paid up to date"? And what about kids? How can someone tell their little boy and girl that their Daddy won't be around to play with them for very much longer?

I'm glad that I'm single. I've been too busy working and trying to get promotion to enjoy myself and make any real friends. I've not had a steady girlfriend for about five years now. It's just as well Mum and Dad are dead and our Colin is miles away, in Australia. I never got on very well with Colin anyway. Must be eight years since I saw him last. He's not going to care if I drop dead now or not. No one is going to mourn for me when I go.

No good feeling sorry for myself, that's not the way to live the last six months of my life. I'll have to give up my job I suppose. Can't go on working if I'm going to be in continuous pain. All that working hard for promotion wasted. It's not going to do me any good now. Eighteen years of hard work down the drain. I might as well have a drink, I suppose. I've got some brandy somewhere. I've not drunk spirits much before, usually only drunk them for medicinal purposes. Still, it's not going to do me any harm now. I've got a pain in my chest now. Could be the booze I suppose. No, it's definitely a pain. I'd better take some of those tablets that the good doctor gave me.

What's that ringing noise? Sounds like church bells, but on a Tuesday night? They're getting very loud. Too loud. RRRRRNNNNNGGGG! RRRNNNGGG! Tony woke up in bed, the blankets kicked to the floor and the alarm clock ringing loudly.

"Christ!" exclaimed Tony. "What a bloody horrible dream to have." He silenced the ringing alarm clock and got out of bed.
"Now for some breakfast," he said to himself. As he got to the bottom of the stairway a large, brown envelope came through his letterbox. Then he remembered. He was waiting for some test results from the hospital.

Bill Lunn

I started writing short stories and poems about four years ago when I started attending Adult Education Classes. I thought it would be a good idea to educate myself a bit more because I was out of work and thought that gaining a few qualifications would help me get a job, which it did do. I now have a good job which is hard work but pays well.

I wrote *Thoughts In A Dream* while studying for GCSE English. I had to write about ten or twelve short stories, and although *Thoughts In A Dream* was not one of the stories I submitted for my exam, I was happy to submit it to Gatehouse for possible inclusion in *Telling Tales*.

‡*Bill takes the 'dream formula' and neatly catches us out, with an ending that is a beginning ... He concentrates on one character, and creates Tony's distraught state of mind. He does this through the conversation Tony has with himself, an 'inner monologue', which lasts for most of the story. Do you think this works well in creating Tony's mounting panic?*

Have you tried the 'it was only a dream' formula? It's hard to be original and different within this formula. Bill uses it, and immediately twists it in a neat way. Do you agree?

Is this a tale you can read more than once, or just once?

THE SNOWQUEEN
Victor Grenko

Winter shapes and fashions her beautiful majestic ice-jewels, and uncoils and scatters her storehouse of frozen treasure across the land. The gems sparkle with a rainbow-coloured, brilliant ice-cold winter fire.

Snowflakes that sparkle like diamond rings, and fall and die on the snow, like soldiers on a battlefield. Blue sapphire and turquoise frozen ice lakes engraved with the silver rings of the skaters. Topaz yellow gold church domes that glitter in the bright sunlight of love. Tall emerald green christmas trees that are carved from jade. Ruby red hot fires that heat and warm the cold hand and the cold heart. Amethyst coloured purple spiders' webs glistening silver white and pure raindrop white.

The magic of winter, the slow musical dance of the icicles. They tinkle with a sweet ring and sparkle a brilliant diamond white. The cold bitter wind carries a death sword made of snowstorms and blizzards. Do you hear his cruel howling cry, as he sweeps by? The winter is a rainbow of all the colours, an immortal ice-diamond the Snowqueen wears on her finger. Do you see the beautiful winter palaces, the cruel ice domes, the lost snowcastles inside her cold ice ring? How forgotten they look, how lonely, how still, how sad. Suddenly the ring sparkles with a brilliant red glow. See the children roasting their toes in front of an open

roaring fire, and ice fairies casting giant shadows on the wall as they dance in front of candles, glowing in the dark.

The frozen gems of winter melt into worthless water and Baba* Winter is packing her bags with the first sign of spring. Come back again, Baba Winter, and don't forget your white carpets when next we meet, because winter can be so pretty and so sweet.

*Baba: Russian grandmother.

Victor Grenko

Photo: Marian Keen

My name is Victor Grenko. I go to various adult writing groups in a hospital, colleges and day centre. I am intrigued by the fascinating shapes of letters and the sounds of uttered words. I am an artist, poet and story teller who walks across the empty stage of your heart.

‡*There is something very skilful going on in **The Snowqueen**. Victor uses colours, light, the names of precious stones and other clues that make connections and suggestions for us, to pile up images of a very cold winter. Victor is an artist, as well as a writer. His illustrated book, **A Guide To The Monsters Of The Mind** was published by Gatehouse in 1991. In **The Snowqueen** he gives us colours through words rather than paint.*

What do you see or feel after reading his writing? Is this different from the way you often feel during a very cold winter? How does this writer create 'atmosphere'? When you write, do you ever set out to build up 'atmosphere' for the reader? Do you do it differently?

A TESTING TIME

Mary Corr

My friend
went for his motor-bike test.
The tester said "Drive around,
and when I step out
do your emergency stop".

After fifteen minutes
an ambulance flashed past.

An hour later,
my friend stopped at the test centre.
They said, "Sorry,
the tester stepped in front of
the wrong motor-bike."

Mary Corr

Photo: Marian Keen

I do a bit of work at Rackhouse Centre, in Manchester. We are doing work on newspapers and headlines at the moment, and horoscopes and your stars.

I just thought of *A Testing Time*, and my tutor wrote it down for me. Then I typed it on the computer. I hope you like it.

‡*Do you have a funny story like Mary's that you could write about, or get a 'right hand' to write about for you?*

TURNING POINT
Anne Comrie

Paula walked quickly from the house, suitcase in hand before her courage deserted her, and she retraced her steps. She had broken free from the chains that had made her a prisoner for twenty years. Clutching her suitcase tightly, she walked quickly to the bus-stop, not without a few curious glances from passers-by, which is inevitable with such a large suitcase. "Holidays or hospital?" they must think, as she boards the bus.

On reaching her destination, she got off at the bus stop. Finding the street, she saw a large house with an attic and cellar, of the type used by the gentry in bygone days, but now let off into bedsits and offices. On reaching number six, she walked nervously up the path, wondering whether she had done the right thing. No! she would not give in, now she had reached her goal. She rang the bell three times as she had been instructed to do, and waited tensely, wondering what kind of reception she would receive, remembering the various stories she had heard about these places. A plump woman of about forty, with a smiling face, opened the door and asked her name, and invited her into a long hallway, leading into a large kitchen and put the suitcase down on the floor. Everywhere there seemed to be activity, women chattering, children playing, and nobody seemed to notice her. A cup of tea was given to her, a lifesaver in any situation, she thought. A tiny black girl, of about two came and sat upon her knee. She cuddled the tiny body to her, and immediately felt at home.

"Would you like me to help you upstairs with your suitcase?" one of the women asked.

"Yes please", said Paula. A wave of tiredness swept over her, and her head whirled with doubts and fears. Had she done the right thing? Could she cope? She had been so decisive when she left, but now her courage seemed to have deserted her. The other woman seemed to know instinctively how she felt. "My name is Pat. This place is not so bad when you get used to it. Considering the conditions we are living under, we get on very well together. You need plenty of tolerance, and a sense of humour is vital if you are to survive. It just depends on how bad the conditions are that you have been living under. Some are really horrific but no doubt you will be hearing about these in due course". Pat led her into a tiny attic room with a skylight, and a small window where the sunlight struggled to come through. Four beds lay haphazardly across the room. Paula heaved a sigh of relief. At least she would not be on her own. Gratefully she sank onto the bed, and looked at the clear blue sky visible through the skylight. Had she really made her break, or was it a dream? One thing was sure, no matter what happened she would never go back, but follow this new road no matter where it would lead. Her tiredness got the better of her, and thankfully she sank into a deep, dreamless sleep.

Anne Comrie

Photo: Marian Keen

My problem is finding some peace and quiet to concentrate and write. This television and video age does not allow for peace and quiet, and I begin to wonder if people are actually frightened of it.

Sometimes I have trouble finding inspiration, but I could write a book about the people I know, all with their individual stories to tell, and their unique personalities, every one a story in their own right.

‡*This story is more 'reader-active' than usual. You'll have seen how Anne holds back some information about her character Paula and her 'destination', so that readers must supply it for themselves. Does 'guesswork' make a story more interesting?*

VACANT POSSESSION

Carol Millbanks

In the village of Sunnydale, there was a little cottage by a stream. No one knew about this cottage until Mr and Mrs Harper became tenants.

One dark and dismal night when they were sitting by the fireside sipping their cups of tea, they heard footsteps coming down the pine-wood staircase. When they went to investigate the noise, there was nobody to be seen. They looked in amazement at each other as they wandered back to the sitting room. The door swung shut behind them, and this made a clanking sound. The rain lashed at the window pane. They became apprehensive about the noises and decided to investigate outside.

Mr Harper told his dear wife to 'stay put' in the house, while he went outdoors. His wife told him not to be too long, because of the weather turning so bad. When Mr Harper went down the stone steps at the back of the cottage, there was a man stood there in a black cloak. His head was covered, so it was quite difficult to get an image of him.

Mr Harper asked him what his reason was for being there.

"I am the Spirit of Sunnydale Cottage. I have been appearing here on the first of every month for two hundred years."

Mr Harper stood there, his knees knocking, as he went hot and cold. He answered in a whispering voice,

"You're having me on. You've got to be joking. I m-m-m-mean I've never met a ghost in my life before."

"Well, you have now, chum."

Mr Harper said, "How do I answer that one?"

"By inviting me in for a cup of coffee," said the ghost.

"Well yes, but let me go and tell Mary my wife first. Tell me what your name is, because I can't keep saying 'the ghost'."

"My name is Byer. But let me warn you, before you go back and tell your wife, that I don't walk into any house, I just appear at one of the fireplaces."

"Why is that?" Mr Harper asked.

"Because it's warmer that way. It gets very cold, with the easterly winds coming out every time I am due for a visit, and I am getting fed up with it. That is why I have made a resolution to be near a fire at the time I make a visit. In ten minutes I will appear in your cottage. So, Mr Harper, you had better get your skates on."

Richard went up the steps to the back door, and pushed it open. Mary was stood at the window looking for him.

"Where have you been? I have been so worried. Was

61

it the wind making strange noises, or was it a tree that uprooted in the woods at the back?"

"No my dear, sit down and I will tell you about it. When I went down the stone steps into the valley at the back of our cottage, I met a person, or was it a person?"

"What do you mean Richard? Was it a person or wasn't it? It's got to be one or the other"

"Well, my dear, it's got to be the other then, because it was a ghost"

"Now Richard, have you been to the Dog and Partridge?"

"No dear, honestly, I've not been drinking spirits, I've been seeing them. It's the ghost of Sunnydale. Byer is his name, and I've invited him back for coffee."

"You've what? Am I hearing you right? I think I had better send for the doctor, you're sickening for something."

"No, no I am perfectly alright."

A sudden flash of lightning made the lights dim for a few seconds. At the same time, a gust of wind down the chimney sent smoke into the room. When it cleared, Byer was standing near the fireplace. Mary nearly fell over backwards as this figure appeared.

"I am Byer, the ghost of Sunnydale. I appear ...."

"Just a minute," said Richard, "we're not going through all that again."

As Mary got herself together, she said to Richard,

"This cottage is going up for sale, first thing tomorrow morning."

"But dear, we've only just moved in."

"I don't care, I couldn't share my life with a ghost."

Byer answered, "But I am very friendly and house trained, and I only come once a month."

But Mary refused to be friends.

The next day, the cottage went up for sale. Soon after the 'For Sale' sign went up, a cloaked figure went into the building society on Sunnydale High Street and enquired about the property. He offered a good price for Sunnydale Cottage. He gave his name as Mr Byer.

Carol Millbanks

Photo: Marian Keen

I am a very outgoing type of person and writing short stories for a hobby gives me a great sense of satisfaction and pleasure. I hope you enjoy my story.

‡*Have you ever written a ghost story? If you have, you'll know that it takes a lot to surprise or scare readers. You might end up making them smile, when you planned to scare them! How does Carol get round this in* **Vacant Possession**?

What's your interpretation of the story? Have you written tales in which there's more than one interpretation for readers to make?

Can you tell what kinds of people Mary, Richard and Byer are, from the things they say? What do you learn of Mary and Richard's relationship from their conversations? Have you ever written about a situation through conversation?

64

LAND OF HOPE

Laurence Roper

Peter Goode

They came along the moorland road, between grey stone walls, a man, his wife, and a ragged troop of bare-foot children, festooned with bundles of belongings. To those that met them along the road it was plain to see, by their dress and their shy and diffident manner, that they had come from the country. Their country was not these rough moors, but a place where the earth was put to the plough and there were harvests to gather. The people in these parts were well used to such sights. Ever since the first mill was built down in the next valley a procession of strangers had passed this way, drawn by the promise of unlimited employment. The wandering pedlars brought the news that much the same was happening all along the western side of these bleak hills. A great migration was taking place, towns were blossoming in spots where once there were only a few isolated cottages. Agricultural labourers and artisans from all points of the compass were building a new society, a factory based, urban society.

Little Tommy Towley strode manfully along pausing only now and again to shift the weight of his burden over to the other shoulder. He was hungry, they were all hungry, and had been so since they left the farmland behind. There they had been able to grab potatoes and other root crops from the fields to fill their empty bellies, but up here nothing grew, not even a tree. The loneliness of this empty moorland frightened him, and the prospect of spending the night here filled him with terror. In the fields of home where he had spent his days chasing the crows and the starlings away from a field of swelling grain, the sounds of an abundant nature were all around. Here there was only the lonely cry of the curlew, the sound of sheep, and the whisper of the breeze. The road wound forever upward, but maybe, Tommy thought hopefully, they might reach the summit when they rounded the next bend.

The family came to a halt in time, at a spot where so many others had done before, to gaze in awe at the first sight of their future home. The original mill, and its larger neighbour, were built at the head of the valley in order to harness the full force of the stream that poured down from the moors. Both of these factories, being a mere two storeys high and built in the local stone, were in keeping with the landscape. The workers' red brick dwellings assuredly were not. They were built with rigid conformity in long, straight rows,

66

huddled together back to back, with a steaming midden at each end. This still-growing town which, with the valley bottom filled, was now marching up the hillside, was pleasing to the family however, for no habitation here was as bad as the hovel they had lived in. Their eyes took this in at a glance, for downstream, on the edge of the town, surrounded by a forest of scaffolding, a new mill of colossal size was being built. It gleamed in new red brick, with tiny panes of new glass reflecting the sunlight in the ranks of tall narrow windows. Yet another floor was rising, adding to the four floors already built. All this was dwarfed by the structure being built at its end. Encased within its own narrow network of poles, planks and ladders, the factory chimney was growing at twice the rate of the building it would serve. It was thrusting up towards the clouds. Around this part of the town men worked in a fever of activity. Even the valley road was busy with heavy freight wagons pulled by teams of draught horses, but the streets of the town held only children at their play.

The weary family cast off their burdens a full two hours later, and drank thirstily from the town well, savouring the coolness of the sweet mountain water. After they had drunk their fill and replenished their water containers, they still lingered, hoping to see someone who could advise them of a place where newcomers were welcome. Meanwhile the little ones, worn out by the journey, slept in the sun.

Peter Goode

After a while there came a whiff of the most enticing aroma, the heavenly smell of new-baked bread, torturing them in their hunger. It came from the open door of a house, in which they could glimpse a few sacks and a pair of scales on a rough plank counter. It was some kind of shop. Unnoticed by the others, the father drew a small sack from beneath his smock, took out two copper coins, and marched over to the shop. The money had been given to him by his brother before they set out, for a very necessary purpose.

Without a coin in his pockets, a family such as they, homeless wanderers, could be arrested and charged with vagrancy. The law had always frowned on those who chose to break their bondage to their master, but as he had discovered, this law was little used nowadays. Now the coins would buy food.

Bread had always been a luxury to them, even though they had lived in the midst of plenty. It was made from the grain the family gleaned after the harvest. They enjoyed this heavy black bread cooked in the ashes of the fire, for only a few weeks of the year. They had never tasted yeast-risen bread. They were not to taste it now, for the breadwinner came out of the shop without it. In his kerchief he carried a little oatmeal, which was all he could afford, and the information that there was a place where new-comers camped up on the hillside, past where the latest row of houses was being built. Instantly the family picked up their bundles and followed him as he led the way.

Even before they reached the spot, the farm labourer had received an offer of a job from the foreman on the house-building. It was day work, and the eighteen pence he would come home with tomorrow night would feed them well.

Crude shelters were pitched all about. They were much like their own, a framework of willow rods covered with the cloths in which they carried their belongings. As in the town, only young children could be seen. They were busy blowing their cooking fires into flames, and adding small pieces of sawn timber from the heap they had gathered. As soon as the man chose their spot, a patch of yellowed grass under the lee of the wall, the children dropped their loads and ran back the way they had come to gather their own fuel.

Everyone had their appointed task, the woman to cook, and her husband and her eldest, Jim, the putting up of the shelter. The mother got out her pot, the bowls and the spoons and the dry kindling they always brought with them. A tiny tot brought a blazing brand from his own fire and shyly offered it to the woman. By the time her own children returned with their wood, the tinder was well alight, and soon flames were licking merrily around the sides of her pot.

While they were busy they heard a bell rung in each of the mills, and they turned their eyes towards them. Then as the mill gates opened they heard for the first time the sound that could only be heard in a mill town. This was a sound they would hear night and morning from now on. It was a clatter of clogs on cobbles, as a cheerful army of mill workers heading homeward brought the town to life.

A little while later the menfolk appeared, bringing with them on their clothes the signs of their labours: mortar, stone dust and sawdust from the building work. This was only temporary work that would keep them going until they secured a more permanent job. Then later the women and the working youngsters began to appear, cotton fluff on their clothing. Each returning family brought the day's provisions with them in baskets and cloth-covered basins. Eyes agog, the children watched what went into their cooking pots. Potatoes and vegetables were first prepared and put into the vessels, then, from the basins, they produced good red meat. It was a rich, nourishing meal the others were to eat tonight.

Except for an occasional gift of a piece of fatty bacon, the family had never tasted meat. Savage penalties awaited any starving wretch who dared to take what was not his by right, even a rabbit. Everything, even the wild creatures belonged to those who owned the land. To the land-owning gentry, who demanded only servitude from those beneath them, the common man was of less value than an animal. It was not so here, marvelled the father, where a day's wages kept a family well fed.

The thin gruel was judged ready and the mother doled it out into the waiting wooden bowls according to custom. Her husband, the wage-earner, got the lion's share, followed by the children, then with the scrapings of the pot she spooned out her own minute portion. It all disappeared in a flash, the bowls licked clean, and with nothing more to keep their sleepy eyes open for, the two smallest children fell asleep. The mother ordered them all to rest, and they needed no second bidding for all their eyelids drooped with fatigue. Carrying the sleeping ones with them they retired to the shelter, and cuddled together for warmth on the bare earth, closed their eyes. There was an air of contentment on their pinched faces that night, for they knew they would never starve again.

It was the end of the day, the end of wandering, a day they would remember all their lives, filled with a promise of a bright tomorrow for Tommy and his brothers and sisters. It was not so for their parents. They sat by the fire patiently waiting for the others to finish their meal and send their own children to their sleep. Then, unencumbered, they would all mingle together and talk, find new friends, and profit by the experience of others. In sheer desperation they had taken to the road, not knowing what they would find, but here in this land of opportunity the seeds of ambition had already been sown.

Five years later the family shut the door of their home for the very last time. They had no further use for it. Their sticks of furniture had been sold, they had said their goodbyes to staunch friends and friendly neighbours, and up in the

Peter Goode

graveyard, to the mother who had died in childbirth and the two young ones who had been taken by the typhus. The town was grimy now, the air fouled by smoke, most of it from the tall chimneys of the two big mills that were now the main employers. Shouldering their belongings, they set off once more. Their possessions were scarcely more, nor better, than those they had come with, for they had saved their money diligently.

They were not walking far, only to the next town. From there they would board a train on the new railway and speed through the smoke-filled towns until later that day, they would arrive where a forest of masts clustered around the quays. From the same small money bag that had held the two precious copper coins, Tommy's father woud pay the passage money in golden sovereigns to the master of one of these tall ships.

Life in this world of industry had not lived up to its first golden promise. They had all been slaves, slaves to the unrelenting rhythm of a machine. Life had become cruel and hard, especially to Tommy and the young ones. They were all pale-skinned from their days in the mill, but they would soon be tanned and healthy again. They were going to a new land, where it was said, all men were free. Another land of promise beckoned them, where men could claim their own territory and be their own master. The seeds of ambition were about to bear fruit, and there was laughter now in their voices.

Laurence Roper

Photo: Marian Keen

This story began life at a Gatehouse writers' workshop held in March '88. It almost died a natural death afterwards, for I couldn't find a way to finish it. The last few sentences had been typed three weeks ago and the paper, still in my portable, was beginning to wilt. When Ursula Howard asked our group to write a short story about life in Victorian times, I rattled off a page without even a pause. It looked very promising. I believed I had even managed to write it in a style suitable to the times I was writing about. It worried me that I couldn't finish it. I was supposed to send it off to

Gatehouse. Even at that point I thought I might be too late, if by some miracle I managed to think of an ending.

Bill, sitting beside me in the adult basic education class, produced that week a well thought out and delightful piece about his native Northenden, that would certainly be included in our class magazine at the end of term. Write about something you know, that was good advice. With *Land of Hope* there didn't seem to be much hope. I had bitten off more than I could chew.

Then, although I was busy doing something else at the time which had its own special problems, the solution suddenly came to me. Two days later on my last sheet of typing paper, now well plastered with 'Tipp-Ex', I finished the story. I expect there were more than a few mistakes but it would have to do. In the post it went that night. I never would have thought then that one day I would see it in print.

‡*The polished 'finish' to this story disguises a lot of thinking and re-working. Laurence gives us an interesting story and accurate historical background. He uses long sentences and formal words. As he tells us, this is partly because he is trying to write the way people used to write, in the time he is writing about.*

This story might make you look in your dictionary for a couple of words. Is this good or bad? Does the writer hold your interest? How? Do you think he has used any of his own experience in a story such as this, or is it all imagination?

A DAY AT BLACKPOOL

The 21 Hour Group

CHARACTERS:

STEVE & JOHN .... TWO TRENDY YOUNG FELLAS

ANNE & VIV .... TWO TRENDY YOUNG SISTERS

MR ROBINSON, MRS ROBINSON .... PENSIONERS

PARKER .... LIFT CASHIER

SCENE ONE: ENTRANCE TO LIFT, BLACKPOOL TOWER.
(Boys approach lift. Girls already inside).

STEVE   Come on John, let's get this lift. Here's
               our big chance.

JOHN   I fancy that blonde one.

STEVE   How much, mate?

PARKER   50p each. We'll call it a pound for the
               two of you. It must be your lucky day.

          (Lads pay up and go through turnstile).

ANNE	Hey Viv, look at these two lads coming in the lift! I fancy the one with the dark hair. You can have the one with the long white legs.
VIV	Thanks very much, Sis.
MRS ROBINSON	Hold the lift! Hold the lift!
PARKER	Alright dear, don't lose your false teeth.
MR ROBINSON	We're doing our best. We're not spring chickens any more.
MRS ROBINSON	How much is it for senior citizens, young man?
PARKER	Two for the price of one. That'll be 50p, ten bob to you.
JOHN	Crikey, here comes gran and grandpa. We're not going to be able to get up to much now. There goes the chance of a lifetime.

SCENE TWO: INSIDE THE LIFT.

STEVE   I can't stand the feeling I get when
                   lifts start off. I wish I had someone to
                   hold on to.

JOHN   Don't look at me! Grab the grannie.

MR ROBINSON   Hey, don't you be so cheeky young
                   man. I'm not too old to give you a
                   thick ear.

VIV (TO JOHN)   That put you in your place didn't it?

    (John blushes, then there is a grinding sound)

VIV   Hey! What's that noise?

ANNE   We should have brought the can of
                   '3 in 1' with us.

(Suddenly the lift judders and comes to a halt. There is
                   a moment of shocked silence)

JOHN   Are we there? (He steps forward)

MR ROBINSON   Hang on son, we're not there yet.

ANNE	So why have we stopped?
MRS ROBINSON	We must have broken down, love.
STEVE	Oh no!
VIV	Do something!
ANNE	Like what?
JOHN	Like putting a new battery in it.
VIV	Don't be so stupid!
MR ROBINSON	Keep calm. Keep calm. There must be an alarm button.

SCENE THREE: PANIC IN THE LIFT

STEVE	There it is. Just press it, anyone.

(Anne presses the button).

STEVE	Nothing's happened! Why hasn't anything happened?
MR ROBINSON	Give them time lad.

(Viv starts to weep)

VIV   We could be stuck up here all day.
                       Fine day trip this has turned out to be.

ANNE   Don't be so stupid. They won't leave
                       us up here forever. Somebody else
                       will want to use the lift.

(Lift suddenly jerks to a start and begins to go down).

STEVE   My God, the cable must have
                       snapped. We're dropping down the
                       shaft.

MRS ROBINSON It's alright son, we're only going down.
                       They've got it working again.

JOHN   Great!

VIV   It's more than great.

ANNE   The sooner we are out the better.

(Lift stops at the bottom. Doors open)

PARKER   Sorry about that little hiccup folks. It all
                       helps to make it a bit more exciting.

	When you're ready, we'll try again at no extra cost.
STEVE	No thanks mate.
VIV	I could do with a strong coffee.
JOHN	I know a great little cafe round the corner.
ANNE	What are we waiting for?

(Mr & Mrs Robinson stay in the lift)

PARKER	Taking advantage of my special offer folks?
MRS ROBINSON	Indeed we are.
MR ROBINSON	The trouble with the younger generation is that they've got no backbone.
PARKER	You're right there! Any more for the joy ride?

A DAY AT BLACKPOOL
The 21 Hour Group

Photo: Marian Keen

Colwyn Dix and Amer Salam from The 21 Hour Group

This is a play written to be read aloud and performed. It was written by the 'Twenty One Hour Group' at the Abraham Moss Community Education Centre. Having decided to write a play that was funny and light, we sat around a table and pooled our ideas. We wanted a link with a happy occasion, a trip, in the spring. The number of people in our group suggested the number of characters. We brainstormed about these characters. Each one was built up in detail, including what they might look like. For example, we were sure that 'Steve' had white legs!

As the story unfolded, it was written down by David, one of our group who was also involved in drama. The bravado of youth, the common sense of pensioners – these were things we tried to get into the dialogue. Everyone's ideas were accepted, then we worked through to a final version that satisfied everyone. After several sessions the play was completed. Two members of the group put it onto a word processor. After this we enjoyed performing it!

Khadiga Alkolani, Gina Barnes, Kevin Barry,
Jean Byrnes, Colwyn Dix, Wayne Jones, Yvonne Jones,
David E. Mahon, Val March, Amer Salam,
Adrian Thompson.

‡*What's different about writing a play? How much do you need to include, when the story is told mostly through dialogue? What kinds of situations lend themselves to play writing? Could any other tale in this book be adapted into a play? What are the 'conventions' for writing plays down?*

NO FRIENDS LIKE OLD FRIENDS

Kathleen Byrne

Ian Hering

Telephone rings .... is picked up .... a bored voice
says ...

"He..llo.... Proudie speaking .... Who? ...... George
Who? .. Oh, ... of course I remember .... Yes .... Fine ...
(warily) .. And you? .. Yes, yes, it has been a long time
.... All of ... well, yes it must be .. I suppose .... Look
George, can't talk now, you know how it is .... I think

not, Georgie, old boy .... Sorry and all that .... But you have rather caught me on the hop .... Just back from Edinburgh .. bit jet-lagged, ha, ha .... Leave me your number .. I'll get my secretary to give you a buzz some time next week .... I try to keep an evening free sometimes ... Dashed hard you know .... On the board now, you know .... not much time for socialising .... 'cept for business, of course ..... Well .. I'm sorry, Georgie, old boy .... What?.. Oh ... Of course I remember you calling ... About two years ago was it? ..... My, how time does fly ...... Well, you see Georgie .. Ah, I remember now, ... I was suddenly called to Liverpool .... really quite urgent business .... But I am sure my secretary was told to .. er .... You didn't get any message? ..... Oh, dear, sorry about that but we really had no vacancies, George .... Still don't ..... You must know how tight things have been for the past few years ... It means an increased workload for the likes of me, of course, but ..... Oh, you aren't? You got fixed up then? ... Good .... Good ... so glad .... Computers, hey? ... Well, you know, Georgie, we are an old-fashioned firm ... like to concentrate on reliability and personal service .... Oh, she's fine .... still teaching .... Head of the Art Department now ...... How's .. erm .... er ..... yes, Emmie .... Oh, that's nice ...... of course, Sybil could never settle down to total domesticity ...... No, no more .... just the twins ..... We didn't feel that .... we ... you know ... population explosion and all that ...... What's that, two more? .....

Phone rings, is picked up: George. George who. —

Hello, Proudie speaking. Oh! — Oh, hello. --- How are you? Fine, fine (warily) Very well indeed yes, yes, it has been a long time, all of — -- um, what --- yes it must be, I suppose. Well, well -- Oh, she's fine ---- still teaching... head of the Art Department — now ----

How the writing looked at first.

Five altogether? .... My .. you have been productive ..... Full time job for ... er ... Emmie ... kept her at home, what? .... No worries about what she's up to when your back's turned, ha, ha .... Well, nice to talk to you George, I really must go ..

Sara? .... Yes ... she got married last year .... Quite a big affair .... local press played it up for all it was worth .. you know .. Ex-Mayor's daughter weds Harley Street doctor .... Well, no .... not exactly Harley Street but just round the corner ...... Well .. no ... He's a bit young .. but very good prospects ... We were very satisfied .... Quite a catch as they say ..... Ah, Oliver ... Ah ... He's doing very well at college .... Well ... he decided against Cambridge. You know how young people get these ideas .... wanted to be more in touch with grass-roots, he said .... in Manchester .... . not the University exactly ...... It's a private college .... management consultancy ..... seems to know what he's doing at last ..... Quite a boy ... Full of beans .... Believes in living his life to the full ... Young rip ...... Well, leave me your number George, I'll see what I can fit in .... Oh .... really .. (long pause) ... but surely he can't be more than twenty five .... Mm .. twenty four ... so young ... Well .... who would've believed it .... You must be very proud ...... And the others ... How about little Marjorie? ... Of course, I mean Margaret .... Married yet? ...... What! (Really surprised) That little thing in the ballet dress? .... Good Heavens ..... Well, of course I've seen it .. but you know how it is ..... Don't really look at the credits ... 'specially directors and things ..... Well ... who'd've thought it ... (stiffly) Very nice for you George .... I'm very pleased .... Must be quite a relief to you to know they are doing so well ...... James ... Well I never met the others ... He would've been the baby, yes ... Oh ... medical school .... Splendid ... splendid .... still at school, of course .... Well, you've done very well for them, George ..... Sorry about your dinner party ... How long are you staying? .... Mm .. weekend ... Where? the Dorchester? ...... West

End? ... Bit much on expenses old boy, isn't it? ......
(Pause) Oh, ... Your own firm .... We-ell ... Give me
your room number George, ... Er ... Penthouse Suite?
.... Oh, ... Oh .... Quite ..... Er .. .. Well ... Maybe I could
cancel something ..... I see ... Lord Wentworth ....
Frederick Harriman will be there .... Sir Joseph and
Lady Canthorpe ...... Well .... Of course, George .... Oh,
Sybil will be delighted ..... not at all ... not at all ..... lovely
to hear from you .... yes ... seven thirty on the dot .....
Dying to hear all your news, ... No friends like old
friends, hey? ...... Bye, George .... See you tonight."

Telephone is replaced.

...... A short line of dots shows a pause.

Kathleen Byrne

Photo: Marian Keen

I used to like writing when I was a child. About the age of say, nine or ten, I would write sentimental little poems about grey-haired old ladies, thatched cottages with roses round the door, beautiful princesses locked in towers, sweet little animals abandoned, that sort of thing. During my teens I was involved in other things, boys, clothes, make-up and so on. Writing took a back seat most of the time, except for some occasional funny verses to amuse friends. Then came marriage and babies and no time for self-indulgent frivolities – how stupid that idea seems now. But middle-age brought a kind of freedom. I was a person just like everyone else. There was a brain inside this head with ideas of its own, no matter how daft they might seem to others. A bit apprehensive, I joined a writers' workshop and haven't looked back. So I may never be rich and famous but who cares. Writing is something I like to do.

I believe everybody can write. It's like singing, dancing or painting pictures. Everyone can do it. It is just that some people do it better than others. If you let the fact that some people will always be able to do something better than you stop you doing it – then you will never do anything.

Almost everyone has a good gossip or interesting conversation some time in the day. Why should it be so easy to chat and yet so difficult to get the same information written down?

‡*We show what we're thinking through what we say and how we say it! In order to write what Proudie says, Kathleen had to know what George said too. Is George's side of the conversation clear to you? What do you think these two men are like? Have you too tried writing a conversation so as to show through what is said, what kind of people are speaking and what they are thinking?*

No Friends Like Old Friends *could be thought of as drama. Do you think it could be performed?*

THE BLANK PAGE

Kathleen Byrne

We all know the feeling. Just as you settle down to write, your mind goes as blank as the page in front of you. All that whiteness of paper, like being lost in the snow. Oh, if I could just get started.

It sounds silly I know, but I find it helps sometimes just to use coloured paper. Not quite so stark, so intimidating. If the mind really needs a jump start, there are a few tricks I use to get it going. For instance, look out of the window. What is the weather like? Write it down. The colour of earth and sky, the shape of buildings, the texture of trees – get them down exactly. Do they remind you of anything? What does the air smell like today? If that does nothing for you, try to imagine the scene around the corner, over the hill, fence or treetop just out of sight. Nearer to home, describe the room you are sitting in, or the room, passageway, whatever, beyond the door.

Perhaps by now you have a few words on that page. Having set the scene, you could now bring in a character, an animal or something else, and get your story going. There are lots of other tricks used by writers to unfreeze that block. What strong emotions have you felt in the past twenty four hours? What have you eaten that was really good, or bad? The most memorable patch of colour, that smell that brought back memories? But that's enough – I am not going to tell you all my secrets, am I?

Gatehouse is a unique publisher.
Our writers are adults who are developing their basic reading and writing skills.

Their ideas and experiences make fascinating material for any reader, but are particularly relevant for adults working on their reading and writing skills.

The books that come from Gatehouse are the work of people whose stories, though worth the telling, would not normally get into print.

Gatehouse books reflect back to the adult learner reader, insights and experiences from other adult students. They work because often the writing strikes a chord – a shared experience of struggling against many odds.

The format of our books is clear and uncluttered. The language is familiar and the text is often line-broken, so that each line ends at a natural pause.

Gatehouse books are both popular and respected within Adult Basic Education throughout the English speaking world. They are also a valued resource within secondary schools, Special Needs education, Social Services and within the Prison Education Service and the Resettlement and Probation services.

They are a bond between writer and reader.

A promise that your story is worth telling too.

A stimulus for more student writing.

For the Gatehouse Book List contact:
Gatehouse Books
Birley Centre, Chichester Road
Manchester M15 5FU. Tel: 061-226 7152